EASY
SPANISH
WORD GAMES
& PUZZLES

Ja

Ma

PASSPORT BOOKS

NTC/Contemporary Publishing Group

PREFACE

Experience has shown that entertaining games and puzzles are effective tools for helping Spanish-language learners (from beginners to advanced) build their vocabulary. Working with puzzles not only expands vocabulary; it also develops a general understanding of the patterns and structures that make up the Spanish language.

The 40 anagrams and acrostics in *Easy Spanish Word Games & Puzzles* are also designed as reading games. They use Spanish exclusively and, when worked out, form common phrases, proverbs, riddles, and literary quotations. At the beginning of each section, you will find sample puzzles and partial solutions.

Comprehensive Spanish-English and English-Spanish vocabularies at the back of the book will help you solve the puzzles, as well as understand the answers. Puzzles in this book have been arranged according to difficulty. This will allow you to choose puzzles according to your interests.

Those who have enjoyed working out and learning from the puzzles in *Easy Spanish Word Games & Puzzles* will also enjoy *Easy Spanish Crossword Puzzles*. These books are available either at your local bookstore or from National Textbook Company, 4255 West Touhy Avenue, Lincolnwood, Illinois 60646-1975 U.S.A.

ISBN: 0-8442-7242-6

Published by Passport Books,
a division of NTC/Contemporary Publishing Company,
4255 West Touhy Avenue,
Lincolnwood (Chicago), Illinois 60646-1975 U.S.A.
© 1985 by NTC/Contemporary Publishing Company

10 11 12 VRS/VRS 0 4

MUESTRA ILUSTRATIVA

Adivine la palabra que completa cada oración;
luego transfiera las letras al cuadro según los
números correspondientes, para formar una frase
en español.

Si no puede adivinar alguna palabra, no se detenga;
pase a la siguiente y llene los espacios que pueda.

PALABRAS PARA BUSCAR:

Uno se baña en el cuarto de **B A Ñ O**.
$$\overline{9}\ \overline{1}\ \overline{16}\ \overline{17}$$

Quien busca, H A L L A.
$$\overline{7}\ \overline{15}\ \overline{10}\ \overline{18}\ \overline{11}$$

El carnicero ___ ___ ___ ___ la carne.
$$\overline{14}\ \overline{6}\ \overline{13}\ \overline{8}$$

Más vale tarde ___ ___ ___ nunca.
$$\overline{2}\ \overline{3}\ \overline{12}$$

Por ___ ___ o por no, yo lo creo.
$$\overline{5}\ \overline{4}$$

EXPRESIÓN
IDIOMÁTICA
PARA
DESCUBRIR:

Si tiene suficientes letras
en el cuadro, usted podrá
adivinar las que faltan para
completar la frase final.

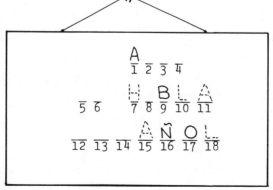

A ___ ___ ___
$$\overline{1}\ \overline{2}\ \overline{3}\ \overline{4}$$

___ ___ H ___ B L A
$$\overline{5}\ \overline{6}\quad \overline{7}\ \overline{8}\ \overline{9}\ \overline{10}\ \overline{11}$$

___ ___ ___ A Ñ O L
$$\overline{12}\ \overline{13}\ \overline{14}\ \overline{15}\ \overline{16}\ \overline{17}\ \overline{18}$$

¡NO LO CREO!

PALABRAS PARA BUSCAR:

Cuatro y cuatro son $\overline{}\ \overline{11}\ \overline{17}\ \overline{10}$.

La $\overline{}\ \overline{15}\ \overline{1}$ mayor es una constelación.

Hace frío en $\overline{14}\ \overline{13}\ \overline{19}\ \overline{9}\ \overline{21}$.

Para ganar en una rifa se necesita $\overline{20}\ \overline{18}\ \overline{7}\ \overline{4}\ \overline{3}\ \overline{16}$.

Perdone usted, $\overline{6}\ \overline{12}\ \overline{8}$ favor.

EXPRESIÓN IDIOMÁTICA PARA DESCUBRIR:

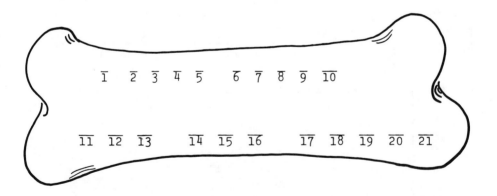

$\overline{1}\quad\overline{2}\quad\overline{3}\quad 4\quad\overline{5}\qquad\overline{6}\quad\overline{7}\quad 8\quad\overline{9}\quad\overline{10}$

$\overline{11}\quad\overline{12}\quad\overline{13}\qquad\overline{14}\quad\overline{15}\quad\overline{16}\qquad\overline{17}\quad\overline{18}\quad\overline{19}\quad\overline{20}\quad\overline{21}$

En los Estados Unidos, lo decimos "Dígalo al juez."

2

¡FIESTA!

PALABRAS PARA BUSCAR:

El compás apunta ___ ___ ___ ___ ___ el norte.
$\quad\quad\quad\quad\quad\quad\quad$ 3 13 9 16 12

De noche, la ___ ___ ___ ___ está en el cielo.
$\quad\quad\quad\quad$ 14 6 11 15

Los ojos son parte de la ___ ___ ___ ___.
$\quad\quad\quad\quad\quad\quad\quad\quad$ 2 4 17 10

Quito es una ciudad ___ ___ el Ecuador.
$\quad\quad\quad\quad\quad\quad\quad$ 1 7

El imperfecto de "soy" es "___ ___ ___."
$\quad\quad\quad\quad\quad\quad\quad\quad$ 18 5 8

EXPRESIÓN PARA DESCUBRIR:

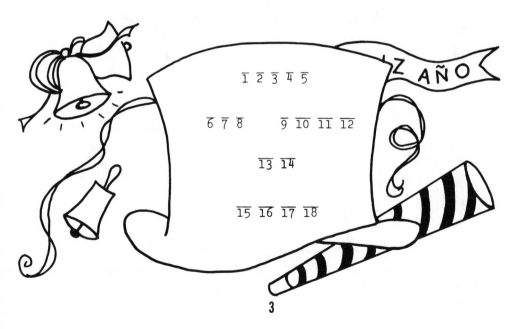

3

Véase la muestra en la página 1	EXPRESIÓN

OTRA COSA

PALABRAS PARA BUSCAR:

Estamos en la __ __ __ __ de clase.
20 7 23 11

__ __ __ __ calor en el verano.
6 22 18 1

La Giralda es una __ __ __ __ __ en España.
15 3 8 16 4

Goldilocks encontró tres __ __ __ __.
19 2 14 5

El participio pasivo de "tener"

es __ __ __ __ __ __.
21 13 10 9 12 17

EXPRESIÓN

PARA

BUSCAR:

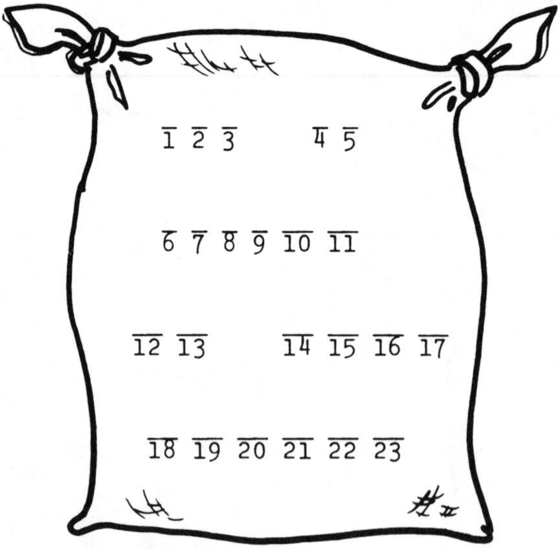

1 2 3   4 5
6 7 8 9 10 11
12 13   14 15 16 17
18 19 20 21 22 23

En los Estados Unidos lo decimos "Un caballo de otro color."

INEPTO

PALABRAS PARA BUSCAR:

Guardo mi dinero en una $\overline{10}\ \overline{7}\ \overline{12}\ \overline{14}\ \overline{18}$ de cuero.

El $\overline{6}\ \overline{1}\ \overline{17}\ \overline{20}\ \overline{16}\ \overline{9}$ Real es una carretera
muy grande.

La sangre de los animales es $\overline{5}\ \overline{11}\ \overline{21}\ \overline{4}$.

El capitán $\overline{8}\ \overline{13}\ \overline{19}\ \overline{3}\ \overline{22}$ en su buque.

Tú no me quieres, $\overline{2}\ \overline{15}$ yo tampoco a ti.

EXPRESIÓN PARA DESCUBRIR:

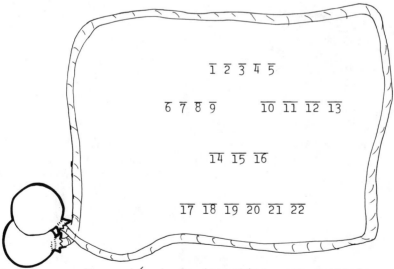

$\overline{1}\ \overline{2}\ \overline{3}\ \overline{4}\ \overline{5}$

$\overline{6}\ \overline{7}\ \overline{8}\ \overline{9}$　　$\overline{10}\ \overline{11}\ \overline{12}\ \overline{13}$

$\overline{14}\ \overline{15}\ \overline{16}$

$\overline{17}\ \overline{18}\ \overline{19}\ \overline{20}\ \overline{21}\ \overline{22}$

Expresión de la Argentina, por supuesto.

5

¡PRONTO!

PALABRAS PARA BUSCAR:

Me gustan éstos más que $\overline{23}\ \overline{12}\ \overline{20}\ \overline{1}\ \overline{24}\ \overline{25}\ \overline{11}\ \overline{7}$.

¿Vienes $\overline{15}\ \overline{6}\ \overline{17}$ migo?

Cristóbal Colón descubrió el nuevo $\overline{3}\ \overline{13}\ \overline{5}\ \overline{8}\ \overline{26}$.

Los niños tiernos $\overline{22}\ \overline{16}\ \overline{18}\ \overline{9}\ \overline{19}\ \overline{2}$ por el suelo.

Los que tienen afición a la lectura, $\overline{10}\ \overline{14}\ \overline{4}\ \overline{21}$ muchos libros.

EXPRESIÓN

PARA

DESCUBRIR:

$\overline{1}\ \overline{2}\quad \overline{3}\ \overline{4}\ \overline{5}\ \overline{6}\ \overline{7}$

$\overline{8}\ \overline{9}\quad \overline{10}\ \overline{11}\quad \overline{12}\ \overline{13}\ \overline{14}\quad \overline{15}\ \overline{16}\ \overline{17}\ \overline{18}\ \overline{19}$

$\overline{20}\ \overline{21}\quad \overline{22}\ \overline{23}\ \overline{24}\ \overline{25}\ \overline{26}$

6

MUY INCÓMODO

PALABRAS PARA BUSCAR:

El $\overline{12}\ \overline{10}\ \overline{4}\ \overline{17}\ \overline{14}\ \overline{27}$ se lleva $\overline{22}\ \overline{19}$ la mano.

Lo contrario de "rubio" es $\overline{8}\ \overline{32}\ \overline{5}\ \overline{1}\ \overline{11}\ \overline{9}$.

La pluma es liviana; el plomo es $\overline{28}\ \overline{24}\ \overline{2}\ \overline{20}\ \overline{26}\ \overline{7}$.

La acción de leer es "la $\overline{23}\ \overline{16}\ \overline{6}\ \overline{3}\ \overline{18}\ \overline{31}\ \overline{25}$."

Antes del examen, hay un $\overline{30}\ \overline{29}\ \overline{21}\ \overline{13}\ \overline{33}\ \overline{15}$.

EXPRESIÓN

   PARA

DESCUBRIR:

$\overline{1}\ \overline{2}\ \overline{3}\ \overline{4}\ \overline{5}$

$\overline{6}\ \overline{7}\ \overline{8}\ \overline{9}\quad \overline{10}\ \overline{11}\quad \overline{12}\ \overline{13}\ \overline{14}\ \overline{15}$

$\overline{16}\ \overline{17}\quad \overline{18}\ \overline{19}\ \overline{20}\quad \overline{21}\ \overline{22}\ \overline{23}\ \overline{24}\ \overline{25}$

$\overline{26}\ \overline{27}\quad \overline{28}\ \overline{29}\ \overline{30}\ \overline{31}\ \overline{32}\ \overline{33}$

Expresión
de
Colombia

7

SUSPICACIA

PALABRAS PARA BUSCAR:

Yo tengo mucha hambre. Creo que es $\overline{}_5 \overline{}_{11} \overline{}_{17} \overline{}_9$ de cenar.

El marido de la reina es sin duda el $\overline{}_{16} \overline{}_{12} \overline{}_7$.

Proverbio antiguo: " $\overline{}_2 \overline{}_3 \overline{}_4 \overline{}_{15} \overline{}_{13}$ tiene dineros, tiene compañeros."

Otro proverbio: " $\overline{}_{14} \overline{}_6 \overline{}_{19} \overline{}_1$ maestra tiene su librito."

Gota a $\overline{}_8 \overline{}_{20} \overline{}_{10} \overline{}_{18}$ se pierde el agua.

EXPRESIÓN

PARA

DESCUBRIR:

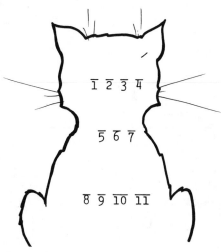

$\overline{1} \overline{2} \overline{3} \overline{4}$

$\overline{5} \overline{6} \overline{7}$

$\overline{8} \overline{9} \overline{10} \overline{11}$

En inglés,

se trata de una $\overline{12} \overline{13} \overline{14} \overline{15} \overline{16} \overline{17} \overline{18} \overline{19} \overline{20}$

rata que uno percibe

HAMBRIENTO

PALABRAS PARA BUSCAR:

Un niño muy pequeño es un $\overline{18}\ \overline{1}\ \overline{26}\ \overline{21}$.

$\overline{12}\ \overline{25}\ \overline{2}\ \overline{3}\ \overline{8}$ Rica es un país de Centroamérica.

Un tambor hace mucho $\overline{5}\ \overline{9}\ \overline{16}\ \overline{19}\ \overline{11}$.

El vaso está $\overline{6}\ \overline{23}\ \overline{17}\ \overline{10}\ \overline{13}$ de leche.

Yo quiero $\overline{22}\ \overline{7}\ \overline{24}\ \overline{14}$ un libro interesante.

El pastor $\overline{20}\ \overline{15}\ \overline{4}$ en su iglesia.

EXPRESIÓN

  PARA

DESCUBRIR:

$\overline{1}\ \overline{2}\ \overline{3}\ \overline{4}\ \overline{5}\ \overline{6}\ \overline{7}$

$\overline{8}\quad \overline{9}\ \overline{10}\ \overline{11}$

$\overline{12}\ \overline{13}\ \overline{14}\ \overline{15}\ \overline{16}\ \overline{17}\ \overline{18}\ \overline{19}\ \overline{20}$

$\overline{21}\ \overline{22}\qquad \overline{23}\ \overline{24}\ \overline{25}\ \overline{26}$

Expresión
del Perú.
En inglés,
"tan hambriento
como un lobo."

9

EXAGERACIÓN

PALABRAS PARA BUSCAR:

El perro es el peor enemigo del $\overline{4}\ \overline{13}\ \overline{16}\ \overline{15}$.

Carlos $\overline{10}\ \overline{23}\ \overline{18}\ \overline{1}$ mucho porque le gusta la natación.

"Estados Unidos" se abrevia" $\overline{8}\ \overline{9}\ \overline{11}\ \overline{22}$."

Los muchachos $\overline{7}\ \overline{19}$ fueron a las dos.

Una compra muy barata es una $\overline{14}\ \overline{17}\ \overline{12}\ \overline{21}\ \overline{5}$.

"El reloj de Jerusalén da la $\overline{2}\ \overline{3}\ \overline{6}\ \overline{20}$ siempre
bien." (Juego de niños)

EXPRESIÓN PARA DESCUBRIR:

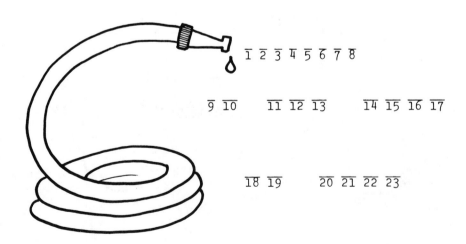

$\overline{1}\ \overline{2}\ \overline{3}\ \overline{4}\ \overline{5}\ \overline{6}\ \overline{7}\ \overline{8}$

$\overline{9}\ \overline{10}\qquad \overline{11}\ \overline{12}\ \overline{13}\qquad \overline{14}\ \overline{15}\ \overline{16}\ \overline{17}$

$\overline{18}\ \overline{19}\qquad \overline{20}\ \overline{21}\ \overline{22}\ \overline{23}$

Véase la muestra
en la página 1

EXPRESIÓN

EXAGERACIÓN NICARAGÜENSE

PALABRAS PARA BUSCAR:

La amiga del muchacho es una 18 8 3 21 15 20 1 10.

Vivo 24 17 una casa vieja.

El niño juega con un 14 16 12 13 4 23 7.

De nada sirve pensar en lo que 22 5 2 y ya no es.

Un cero a la izquierda no vale 9 11 6 19.

EXPRESIÓN

PARA

DESCUBRIR:

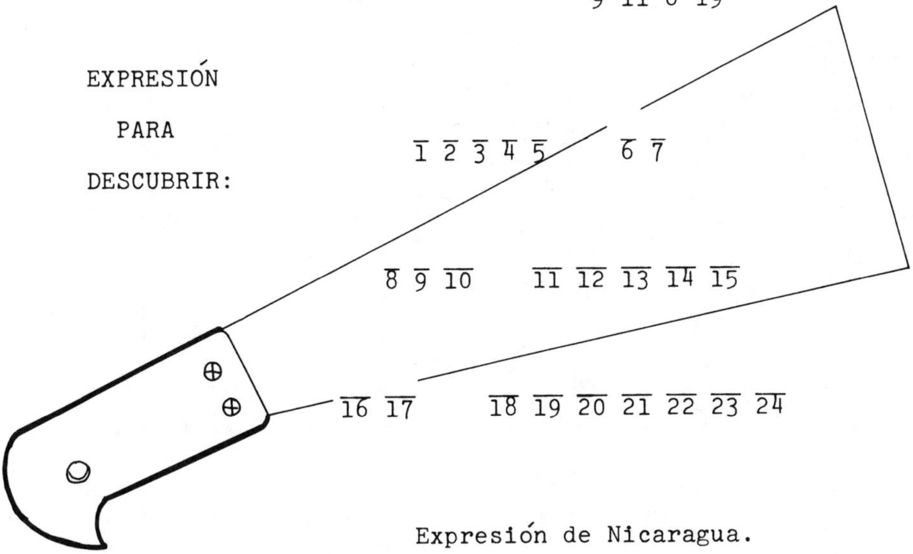

1 2 3 4 5 6 7
8 9 10 11 12 13 14 15
16 17 18 19 20 21 22 23 24

Expresión de Nicaragua.

En los Estados Unidos, "hacemos montañas de las topineras."

Véase la muestra
en la página 1

EXPRESIÓN

¡CULPABLE!

PALABRAS PARA BUSCAR:

Manda esta carta por $\overline{10}\ \overline{19}\ \overline{4}\ \overline{5}\ \overline{17}\ \overline{27}$ aéreo.

El bebé $\overline{8}\ \overline{22}\ \overline{11}\ \overline{7}\ \overline{25}$ cuando tiene hambre.

El $\overline{24}\ \overline{6}\ \overline{26}\ \overline{2}\ \overline{9}$ es una fruta tropical.

Bequita llama a su abuela "$\overline{21}\ \overline{1}\ \overline{12}\ \overline{23}$."

Juan escribe una $\overline{20}\ \overline{18}\ \overline{15}\ \overline{16}\ \overline{13}\ \overline{14}\ \overline{3}$ a María en clase.

EXPRESIÓN

PARA

DESCUBRIR:

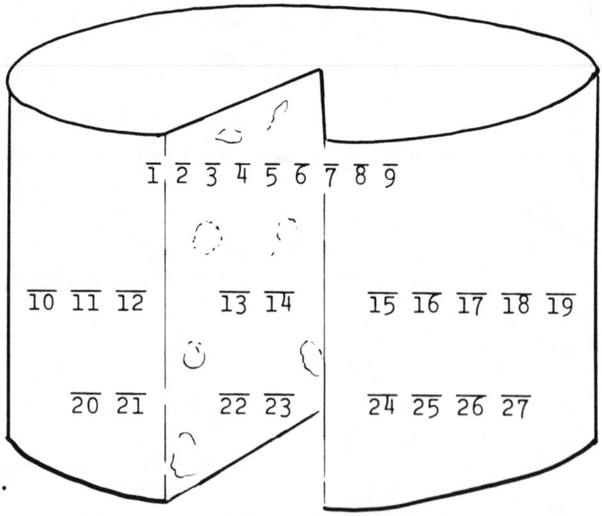

1 2 3 4 5 6 7 8 9
10 11 12
13 14
15 16 17 18 19
20 21
22 23
24 25 26 27

Expresión
de Venezuela.

En los E.E.U.U., el culpable es "agarrado con las manos rojas."

LA PURA VERDAD

PALABRAS PARA BUSCAR:

Yo $\overline{18}\ \overline{21}\ \overline{15}$ si tú también vas.

Las lavanderas $\overline{17}\ \overline{3}\ \overline{22}\ \overline{7}\ \overline{14}$ ropa.

La hembra del pollo es la $\overline{9}\ \overline{25}\ \overline{1}\ \overline{2}\ \overline{13}$.

El pájaro puso su nido en una $\overline{6}\ \overline{16}\ \overline{4}\ \overline{10}$ de un árbol.

El indeciso no dice $\overline{20}\ \overline{23}$ sí, $\overline{24}\ \overline{19}$ no.

Un mapa de una ciudad es un $\overline{12}\ \overline{8}\ \overline{5}\ \overline{11}$.

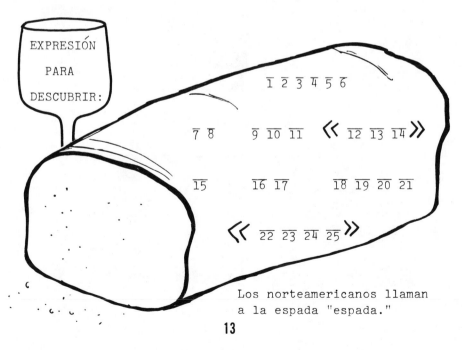

EXPRESIÓN

PARA

DESCUBRIR:

$\overline{1}\ \overline{2}\ \overline{3}\ \overline{4}\ \overline{5}\ \overline{6}$

$\overline{7}\ \overline{8}$ $\overline{9}\ \overline{10}\ \overline{11}$ 《 $\overline{12}\ \overline{13}\ \overline{14}$ 》

$\overline{15}$ $\overline{16}\ \overline{17}$ $\overline{18}\ \overline{19}\ \overline{20}\ \overline{21}$

《 $\overline{22}\ \overline{23}\ \overline{24}\ \overline{25}$ 》

Los norteamericanos llaman
a la espada "espada."

BRINDIS A LA ESPAÑOLA

PALABRAS PARA BUSCAR:

El dólar vale como doce ___ ___ ___ ___ ___ mexicanos.
$\overline{6}\ \overline{9}\ \overline{1}\ \overline{16}\ \overline{12}$

Los alumnos están en la ___ ___ ___ ___ de clase.
$\overline{8}\ \overline{14}\ \overline{3}\ \overline{11}$

Si eres colombiano, eres ___ ___ Colombia.
$\overline{5}\ \overline{7}$

Los barcos navegan por río o por ___ ___ ___.
$\overline{15}\ \overline{2}\ \overline{17}$

Eres mi primo porque ___ ___ madre es mi tía.
$\overline{10}\ \overline{4}$

Carlos ___ María se van a casar.
$\overline{13}$

EXPRESIÓN

 PARA

DESCUBRIR:

$\overline{1}\ \overline{2}\ \overline{3}\ \overline{4}\ \overline{5}$

$\overline{6}\ \overline{7}\ \overline{8}\ \overline{9}\ \overline{10}\ \overline{11}\ \overline{12}$

$\overline{13}$ $\overline{14}\ \overline{15}\ \overline{16}\ \overline{17}$

14

MERECIDO

PALABRAS PARA BUSCAR:

Los novios están en su $\overline{21}\ \overline{24}\ \overline{10}\ \overline{28}$ de miel.

El gato atrapó una $\overline{5}\ \overline{2}\ \overline{27}\ \overline{8}$.

Los malos van al infierno, los buenos al $\overline{23}\ \overline{4}\ \overline{12}\ \overline{6}\ \overline{19}$.

$\overline{18}\ \overline{7}\ \overline{20}\ \overline{16}\ \overline{11}$ que ladra no muerde.

"Luisa" es la forma femenina de "$\overline{3}\ \overline{9}\ \overline{15}\ \overline{1}$."

Cuando me baño, me seco con una $\overline{14}\ \overline{17}\ \overline{22}\ \overline{13}\ \overline{25}\ \overline{26}$.

EXPRESIÓN PARA DESCUBRIR:

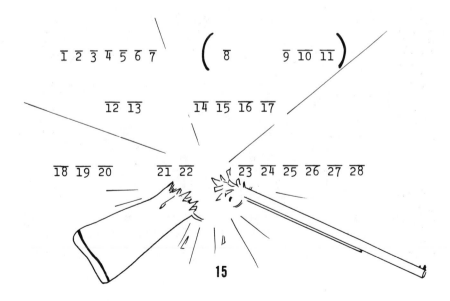

15

BUEN SENTIDO

Para resolver los anagramas que siguen, encuentre las palabras definidas en la columna izquierda, escríbalas en los espacios indicados a la derecha, y luego transfiéralas al pie de la página según los números.

PALABRAS CLAVES:

A. Los semicírculos que forman los pelos situados arriba de los ojos:

C E J A S
19 12 3 20 7

B. Acción del fuego:

Q U E M A R
13 17 15 1 9 10

C. Imperativo plural de "dar":

— — —
11 6 18

D. Ruido fuerte producido en las nubes durante las tormentas:

— — — — — —
8 5 14 2 16 4

El resultado será un proverbio o adagio en español que usted podrá aprender de memoria.

PROVERBIO:

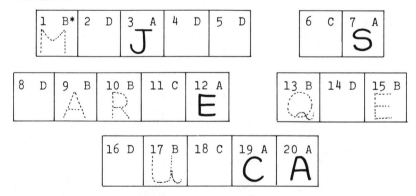

1 B*	2 D	3 A	4 D	5 D		6 C	7 A
M		J					S

8 D	9 B	10 B	11 C	12 A		13 B	14 D	15 B
A	R	R		E		Q		E

16 D	17 B	18 C	19 A	20 A
	U		C	A

*Las letras a la derecha de los números en las casillas corresponden a las letras junto a las definiciones.

Véase la muestra en la página 16	PROVERBIO

PESCADO

PALABRAS CLAVES:

A. Pronombre singular reflexivo de la primera persona: __ __ (10 15)

B. Pronombre reflexivo singular o plural: __ __ (4 14)

C. Cortar el pelo, mondar una fruta: __ __ __ __ __ (1 18 16 9 3)

D. Hombre que trabaja debajo del agua: __ __ __ __ (6 11 19 7)

E. Cerdo: __ __ __ __ __ __ (17 5 12 13 8 2)

PROVERBIO:

1 C	2 E	3 C

4 B	5 E

6 D	7 D	8 E	9 C

10 A	11 D	12 E	13 E	14 B

15 A	16 C

17 E	18 C	19 D

PENSAMIENTO

PALABRAS CLAVES:

A. Nene, niño tierno:

$$\overline{9} \quad \overline{3} \quad \overline{19} \quad \overline{8}$$

B. Sobrenombre:

$$\overline{5} \quad \overline{13} \quad \overline{1} \quad \overline{17} \quad \overline{24}$$

C. Hueso que forma la parte
inferior de la cara:

$$\overline{6} \quad \overline{7} \quad \overline{14} \quad \overline{4} \quad \overline{12} \quad \overline{23} \quad \overline{10}$$

D. Nada (número):

$$\overline{21} \quad \overline{15} \quad \overline{16} \quad \overline{20}$$

E. Cilindro de cera que
sirve para alumbrar:

$$\overline{2} \quad \overline{18} \quad \overline{11} \quad \overline{22}$$

PROVERBIO:

1 B	2 E	3 A	4 C	5 B

6 C	7 C	8 A

9 A	10 C	11 E	12 C

13 B	14 C	15 D	16 D	17 B	18 E

19 A	20 D	21 D	22 E	23 C	24 B

DIVISA PARA ESTUDIANTES

PALABRAS CLAVES:

A. Desear:

$$\overline{13} \ \overline{14} \ \overline{7} \ \overline{12} \ \overline{17} \ \overline{20}$$

B. Asunto, materia:

$$\overline{16} \ \overline{11} \ \overline{1} \ \overline{5}$$

C. Proyectiles de las
   armas de fuego:

$$\overline{10} \ \overline{2} \ \overline{6} \ \overline{9} \ \overline{3}$$

D. Forma de "ver",
   presente (Pl.):

$$\overline{4} \ \overline{15} \ \overline{18}$$

E. Pronombre reflexivo:

$$\overline{8} \ \overline{19}$$

PROVERBIO:

1 B	2 C	3 C

4 D	5 B	6 C	7 A

8 E	9 C	10 C	11 B	12 A

13 A	14 A	15 D

16 B	17 A	18 D	19 E	20 A

HABLADOR

PALABRAS CLAVES:

A. Hebra que se
   usa para coser: $\overline{9}$ $\overline{3}$ $\overline{14}$ $\overline{20}$

B. Niño, mozo:
   $\overline{6}$ $\overline{17}$ $\overline{8}$ $\overline{11}$ $\overline{25}$ $\overline{18}$ $\overline{19}$ $\overline{10}$

C. Adjetivo numeral que
   se usa antes de
   sustantivos masculinos: $\overline{2}$ $\overline{5}$

D. Romper, rajar:
   $\overline{1}$ $\overline{7}$ $\overline{22}$ $\overline{13}$ $\overline{23}$ $\overline{12}$ $\overline{24}$

E. Parte amarilla del
   huevo de ave: $\overline{21}$ $\overline{4}$ $\overline{16}$ $\overline{15}$

PROVERBIO:

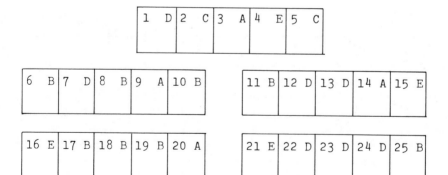

1 D	2 C	3 A	4 E	5 C

6 B	7 D	8 B	9 A	10 B

11 B	12 D	13 D	14 A	15 E

16 E	17 B	18 B	19 B	20 A

21 E	22 D	23 D	24 D	25 B

AVARICIA

PALABRAS CLAVES:

A. Capital del Ecuador:

$\overline{1}$ $\overline{7}$ $\overline{24}$ $\overline{26}$ $\overline{10}$

B. País entre Bolivia
y Ecuador:

$\overline{17}$ $\overline{4}$ $\overline{14}$ $\overline{2}$

C. Parte más alta
de una montaña:

$\overline{8}$ $\overline{3}$ $\overline{6}$ $\overline{21}$

D. Cola de un animal:

$\overline{23}$ $\overline{27}$ $\overline{12}$ $\overline{18}$

E. Prenda de vestir
sin mangas:

$\overline{19}$ $\overline{16}$ $\overline{22}$ $\overline{13}$

F. En la noche de ayer:

$\overline{11}$ $\overline{5}$ $\overline{20}$ $\overline{15}$ $\overline{9}$ $\overline{25}$

PROVERBIO:

1 A	2 B	3 C	4 B	5 F		6 C	7 A	8 C	9 F	10 A

11 F	12 D	13 E	14 B	15 F	16 E		17 B	18 D	19 E	20 F

21 C	22 E	23 D	24 A	25 F	26 A	27 D

DONDE HAY HUMO, HAY FUEGO

PALABRAS CLAVES:

A. Nombre de una
   flor muy común: $\overline{9}$ $\overline{6}$ $\overline{12}$ $\overline{26}$

B. El que escribe poesías:
   $\overline{17}$ $\overline{11}$ $\overline{14}$ $\overline{24}$ $\overline{3}$

C. La mujer del rey:
   $\overline{21}$ $\overline{7}$ $\overline{18}$ $\overline{4}$ $\overline{16}$

D. El primer día
   de la semana: $\overline{8}$ $\overline{13}$ $\overline{15}$ $\overline{27}$ $\overline{23}$

E. Población grande:
   $\overline{1}$ $\overline{10}$ $\overline{2}$ $\overline{20}$ $\overline{22}$ $\overline{5}$

F. Segunda nota de la
   escala musical: $\overline{25}$ $\overline{19}$

PROVERBIO:

1 E	2 E	3 B	4 C	5 E	6 A		7 C	8 D

9 A	10 E	11 B		12 A	13 D	14 B	15 D	16 C

17 B	18 C	19 F	20 E	21 C	22 E	23 D

24 B	25 F	26 A	27 D

22

RECUERDE

PALABRAS CLAVES:

A. Mujer del duque:

$$\overline{13} \quad \overline{4} \quad \overline{3} \quad \overline{10} \quad \overline{18} \quad \overline{16} \quad \overline{19}$$

B. Imperativo de "decir"
   y pretérito de "dar":

$$\overline{8} \quad \overline{14}$$

C. Río de España

$$\overline{22} \quad \overline{21} \quad \overline{5} \quad \overline{9} \quad \overline{15}$$

D. Herida, úlcera:

$$\overline{2} \quad \overline{17} \quad \overline{7} \quad \overline{11} \quad \overline{23}$$

E. Una de las civilizaciones
   aborígenes en Centro América antes de la conquista:

$$\overline{6} \quad \overline{1} \quad \overline{20} \quad \overline{12}$$

PROVERBIO:

1	E	2	D		3	A	4	A	5	C

6	E	7	D	8	B	9	C	10	A	11	D	12	E

13	A	14	B	15	C	16	A

17	D	18	A		19	A	20	E	21	C	22	C	23	D

VENTAJA

PALABRAS CLAVES:

A. Número entre seis y ocho:

$\overline{26}$ $\overline{4}$ $\overline{1}$ $\overline{19}$ $\overline{10}$

B. Pelea entre naciones:

$\overline{14}$ $\overline{20}$ $\overline{17}$ $\overline{6}$ $\overline{22}$ $\overline{8}$

C. Bastón, símbolo de
   autoridad real:

$\overline{11}$ $\overline{27}$ $\overline{3}$ $\overline{29}$ $\overline{24}$

D. El que oye:

$\overline{15}$ $\overline{31}$ $\overline{21}$ $\overline{2}$ $\overline{23}$ $\overline{25}$

E. Los carriles del tren
   o del tranvía:

$\overline{7}$ $\overline{12}$ $\overline{30}$ $\overline{18}$ $\overline{13}$ $\overline{16}$

F. Contracción de la preposición "de" y el artículo
   "el":

$\overline{9}$ $\overline{5}$ $\overline{28}$

PROVERBIO:

1 A	2 D

3 C	4 A	5 F	6 B	7 E	8 B

9 F	10 A

11 C	12 E	13 E	14 B	15 D	16 E

17 B	18 E

19 A	20 B	21 D	22 B	23 D	24 C

25 D	26 A

27 C	28 F

29 C	30 E	31 D

TRISTE VERDAD

PALABRAS CLAVES:

A. Hermoso, lindo:

$\overline{31}\ \overline{25}\ \overline{2}\ \overline{13}\ \overline{18}$

B. El que estudia:

$\overline{10}\ \overline{21}\ \overline{28}\ \overline{27}\ \overline{11}\ \overline{8}\ \overline{30}\ \overline{16}\ \overline{14}\ \overline{20}$

C. Abreviatura de "Usted":

$\overline{7}\ \overline{24}$

D. Anciano; hombre de
   muchos años de edad:

$\overline{5}\ \overline{4}\ \overline{23}\ \overline{33}\ \overline{15}$

E. Lo que hacen los ojos; mirar:

$\overline{9}\ \overline{12}\ \overline{29}$

F. Barco de lujo o de recreo:

$\overline{19}\ \overline{32}\ \overline{22}\ \overline{1}$

G. Lo que dan los ciudadanos
   para elegir al presidente:

$\overline{3}\ \overline{34}\ \overline{17}\ \overline{6}\ \overline{26}$

PROVERBIO:

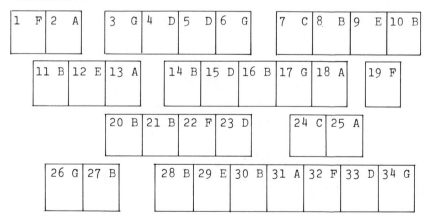

NUNCA DIGAS NUNCA

PALABRAS CLAVES:

A. Lo contrario de "blanco":

$\overline{1}$ $\overline{12}$ $\overline{18}$ $\overline{31}$ $\overline{22}$

B. Tiempo que uno ha vivido:

$\overline{13}$ $\overline{25}$ $\overline{17}$ $\overline{6}$

C. Personas; grupo de personas:

$\overline{8}$ $\overline{24}$ $\overline{3}$ $\overline{15}$ $\overline{30}$

D. Preposición que indica lugar:

$\overline{28}$ $\overline{21}$

E. Entrada del mar en la costa
   similar al golfo:

$\overline{27}$ $\overline{9}$ $\overline{23}$ $\overline{7}$ $\overline{16}$

F. Fundador del Budismo:

$\overline{29}$ $\overline{2}$ $\overline{11}$ $\overline{20}$

G. Mujeres de Suecia:

$\overline{14}$ $\overline{19}$ $\overline{26}$ $\overline{4}$ $\overline{5}$ $\overline{10}$

PROVERBIO:

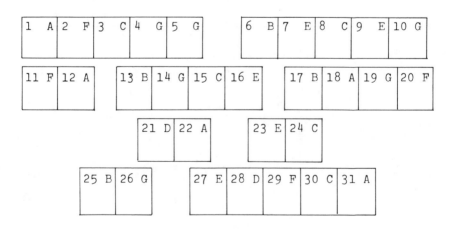

| 1 A | 2 F | 3 C | 4 G | 5 G | | 6 B | 7 E | 8 C | 9 E | 10 G |

| 11 F | 12 A | | 13 B | 14 G | 15 C | 16 E | | 17 B | 18 A | 19 G | 20 F |

| 21 D | 22 A | | 23 E | 24 C |

| 25 B | 26 G | | 27 E | 28 D | 29 F | 30 C | 31 A |

CINISMO

PALABRAS CLAVES:

A. Suma de siete y ocho:

$$\overline{1} \ \overline{2} \ \overline{12} \ \overline{21} \ \overline{23} \ \overline{29}$$

B. Lo que hace la maestra a la clase (con "ella"):

$$\overline{22} \ \overline{13} \ \overline{17} \ \overline{20} \ \overset{\sim}{\overline{28}} \ \overline{27}$$

C. Forma del verbo "perder":

$$\overline{26} \ \overline{3} \ \overline{10} \ \overline{30} \ \overline{11} \ \overline{4}$$

D. Alumnos que ayudan al maestro en la clase:

$$\overline{25} \ \overline{16} \ \overline{9} \ \overline{19} \ \overline{6} \ \overline{31} \ \overline{15} \ \overline{8} \ \overline{32}$$

E. Hijo del hijo o de la hija:

$$\overline{5} \ \overline{7} \ \overline{14} \ \overline{18} \ \overline{24}$$

PROVERBIO:

1 A	2 A	3 C	4 C	5 E		6 D	7 E	8 D	9 D	10 C

	11 C	12 A	13 B	14 E	15 D	16 D	17 B

	18 E	19 D	20 B	21 A	22 B

23 A	24 E	25 D	26 C	27 B	28 B ~	29 A	30 C	31 D	32 D

27

MALOS COMPAÑEROS

PALABRAS CLAVES:

A. Mes que sigue
   mayo: $\overline{15}$ $\overline{22}$ $\overline{5}$ $\overline{3}$ $\overline{12}$

B. Padre del padre
   o de la madre: $\overline{21}$ $\overline{11}$ $\overline{16}$ $\overline{32}$ $\overline{23}$ $\overline{7}$

C. Doce meses: $\overset{\sim}{}$
                           $\overline{19}$ $\overline{33}$ $\overline{10}$

D. Perro: $\overline{6}$ $\overline{20}$ $\overline{17}$

E. Cristales de
   los anteojos: $\overline{9}$ $\overline{14}$ $\overline{8}$ $\overline{18}$ $\overline{29}$ $\overline{31}$

F. Conjunción y
   pronombre relativo: $\overline{1}$ $\overline{2}$ $\overline{28}$

G. Capital de Costa Rica: JOSÉ
                           $\overline{27}$ $\overline{25}$ $\overline{30}$

H. Existir: $\overline{13}$ $\overline{4}$ $\overline{26}$

I. Contracción de la
   preposición "a" y
   el artículo "el": $\overline{34}$ $\overline{24}$

PROVERBIO:

1 F	2 F	3 A	4 H	5 A

6 D	7 B	8 E

9 E	10 C	11 B	12 A

13 H	14 E

15 A	16 B	17 D	18 E	19 C

20 D

21 B	22 A	23 B	24 I	25 G	26 H

27 G	28 F

29 E	30 G	31 E	32 B	33 C ~	34 I

GRATITUD

PALABRAS CLAVES:

A. Reglas de los gobiernos:

$\overline{6}$ $\overline{24}$ $\overline{21}$ $\overline{10}$ $\overline{34}$

B. Macho de la gallina:

$\overline{11}$ $\overline{3}$ $\overline{30}$ $\overline{32}$ $\overline{18}$

C. Cavidad donde están
los dientes y la lengua:

$\overline{4}$ $\overline{8}$ $\overline{2}$ $\overline{28}$

D. Serie de vagones tirados
por una locomotora:

$\overline{39}$ $\overline{9}$ $\overline{40}$ $\overline{17}$

E. Lugar subterráneo de donde
se sacan los minerales:

$\overline{25}$ $\overline{26}$ $\overline{38}$ $\overline{12}$

F. Actualmente*, en
este momento:

$\overline{5}$ $\overline{19}$ $\overline{33}$ $\overline{29}$ $\overline{20}$

G. Carta breve:

$\overline{31}$ $\overline{41}$ $\overline{22}$ $\overline{23}$ $\overline{37}$ $\overline{13}$ $\overline{1}$

H. Voz del perro:

$\overline{7}$ $\overline{14}$ $\overline{35}$ $\overline{27}$ $\overline{36}$ $\overline{15}$ $\overline{16}$

* Recuerde que "actualmente" <u>no</u> significa "actually."

30

PROVERBIO:

1 G

2 C	3 B	4 C	5 F	6 A	7 H	8 C

9 D	10 A	11 B	12 E	13 G	14 H	15 H	16 H

17 D	18 B

19 F	20 F	21 A

22 G	23 G	24 A

25 E	26 E	27 H	28 C	29 F	30 B	31 G

32 B	33 F	34 A

35 H	36 H	37 G	38 E	39 D	40 D	41 G

SABIDURÍA

PALABRAS CLAVES:

A. El día que precede
   al domingo:
   $\overline{4}$ $\overline{2}$ $\overline{13}$ $\overline{32}$ $\overline{30}$ $\overline{23}$

B. Comida popular:
   "arroz con -----":
   $\overline{16}$ $\overline{28}$ $\overline{34}$ $\overline{14}$ $\overline{17}$

C. Tomar un líquido
   por la boca:
   $\overline{33}$ $\overline{21}$ $\overline{6}$ $\overline{26}$ $\overline{29}$

D. Lugares con árboles y
   flores donde la gente
   va de paseo:
   $\overline{27}$ $\overline{12}$ $\overline{18}$ $\overline{24}$ $\overline{25}$ $\overline{8}$ $\overline{3}$

E. Ida de un punto o de
   un país a otro:
   $\overline{19}$ $\overline{11}$ $\overline{5}$ $\overline{22}$ $\overline{7}$

F. Diez por cien
   es igual a ----:
   $\overline{1}$ $\overline{20}$ $\overline{9}$

G. Lo contrario de "amor":
   $\overline{35}$ $\overline{10}$ $\overline{31}$ $\overline{15}$

32

PROVERBIO:

1 F	2 A	3 D

4 A	5 E	6 C	7 E

8 D	9 F

10 G	11 E	12 D	13 A	14 B	15 G

16 B	17 B	18 D

19 E	20 I	21 C	22 E	23 A

24 D	25 D	26 C

27 D	28 B	29 C

30 A	31 G	32 A	33 C	34 B	35 G

Véase la muestra en la página 16

PROVERBIO

MALA INVERSIÓN

PALABRAS CLAVES:

A. Desear, tener cariño: ___ ___ ___ ___ ___ ___ (1 2 13 25 28 37)

B. Niño pequeño: ___ ___ ___ ___ (5 40 10 43)

C. Hoja en que se escribe: ___ ___ ___ ___ ___ (8 17 30 36 41)

D. Pronombre sujeto, primera persona: ___ ___ (33 46)

E. Diosa romana, hija de Júpiter: ___ ___ ___ ___ ___ (38 35 7 20 11)

F. Nombre de la letra N: ___ ___ ___ (24 32 39)

G. Utensilio en que se pone tabaco para fumar: ___ ___ ___ ___ (22 3 42 9)

H. Mujer que tiene el cabello rojo: ___ ___ ___ ___ ___ ___ ___ ___ ___ (12 27 29 23 44 15 16 18 31)

I. Hombre que pierde algo: ___ ___ ___ ___ ___ ___ ___ ___ (34 19 14 6 4 26 21 45)

PROVERBIO:

| 1 A | 2 A | 3 G | 4 I | 5 B |

| 6 I | 7 E |

| 8 C | 9 G | 10 B |

| 11 E |

| 12 H | 13 A | 14 I | 15 H | 16 H |

| 17 C | 18 H | 19 I | 20 E | 21 I |

| 22 G | 23 H | 24 F | 25 A | 26 I | 27 H |

| 28 A | 29 H |

| 30 C | 31 H | 32 F |

| 33 D |

| 34 I | 35 E | 36 C | 37 A | 38 E | 39 F |

| 40 B | 41 C |

| 42 G | 43 B | 44 H | 45 I | 46 D |

¡ADIVINA, ADIVINADOR!

Estos anagramas se resuelven como los
anteriores, pero el resultado será una
adivinanza.

PALABRAS PARA ADIVINAR:

A. Techumbre de una casa:

$$\underset{26}{T}\;\underset{16}{E}\;\underset{7}{J}\;\underset{31}{A}\;\underset{28}{D}\;\underset{10}{O}$$

B. Cintura:

$$\underset{18}{T}\;\underset{3}{A}\;\underset{20}{L}\;\underset{21}{L}\;\underset{36}{E}$$

C. Sustancia blanca que
cae en el invierno:

$$\overline{17}\;\overline{5}\;\overline{33}\;\overline{4}\;\overline{19}$$

D. Lugar que construyen las
aves para poner sus huevos:

$$\overline{11}\;\overline{15}\;\overline{14}\;\overline{27}$$

E. El que ama; querido:

$$\overline{22}\;\overline{23}\;\overline{25}\;\overline{2}\;\overline{35}\;\overline{6}$$

F. Cama de un niño tierno:

$$\overline{9}\;\overline{12}\;\overline{34}\;\overline{8}$$

G. Lago pequeño:

$$\overline{30}\;\overline{24}\;\overline{32}\;\overline{1}\;\overline{13}\;\overline{29}$$

ADIVINANZA PARA ADIVINAR:

36

¡ADIVINA, ADIVINADOR!

PALABRAS PARA ADIVINAR:

A. Alimento hecho de
   harina y ahornado: $\overline{5}$ $\overline{15}$ $\overline{22}$

B. Forma de "dar"--
   segunda persona, presente: $\overline{11}$ $\overline{32}$ $\overline{30}$

C. Forma abreviada
   de "santo": $\overline{13}$ $\overline{27}$ $\overline{35}$

D. País de la
   América Central: $\overline{19}$ $\overline{8}$ $\overline{4}$ $\overline{1}$ $\overline{17}$ RICA

E. Posesivo plural: $\overline{23}$ $\overline{20}$ $\overline{9}$

F. También, además
   (conjunción): $\overline{10}$

G. Pieles rojas de los
   Estados Unidos y del
   norte de Méjico: $\overline{21}$ $\overline{14}$ $\overline{6}$ $\overline{33}$ $\overline{31}$ $\overline{3}$ $\overline{25}$

H. Conjunto de soldados,
   grupo de gente (pl.): $\overline{28}$ $\overline{2}$ $\overline{12}$ $\overline{26}$ $\overline{29}$ $\overline{18}$

I. Expresión familiar que
   significa "detente" o
   "poco a poco": $\overline{16}$ $\overline{24}$ $\overline{7}$ $\overline{34}$

ADIVINANZA PARA ADIVINAR:

¿	1 D	2 H	3 G	4 D		5 A	6 G	7 I	8 D	9 E
10 F		11 B	12 H	13 C		14 G	15 A	16 I	17 D	18 H
19 D	20 E	21 G	22 A	23 E	24 I	25 G		26 H	27 C	28 H	29 H	30 B
31 G	32 B	33 G	34 I	35 C	?	RESPUESTA:

37

¡ADIVINA, ADIVINADOR!

PALABRAS PARA ADIVINAR:

A. El que no cree en Dios:

$\overline{3}$ $\overline{15}$ $\overline{11}$ $\overline{27}$

B. Maleta, baúl de viaje:

$\overline{7}$ $\overline{13}$ $\overline{25}$ $\overline{8}$ $\overline{30}$ $\overline{20}$

C. Persona de poca
inteligencia:

$\overline{28}$ $\overline{18}$ $\overline{23}$ $\overline{5}$ $\overline{16}$

D. Aparato que señala
las horas del día:

$\overline{19}$ $\overline{1}$ $\overline{14}$ $\overline{6}$ $\overline{36}$

E. Relato histórico
tradicional:

$\overline{32}$ $\overline{35}$ $\overline{21}$ $\overline{31}$ $\overline{12}$ $\overline{38}$ $\overline{41}$

F. Roedor parecido al ratón:

$\overline{40}$ $\overline{24}$ $\overline{34}$ $\overline{33}$

G. Forma presente
de "elevar":

$\overline{29}$ $\overline{4}$ $\overline{10}$ $\overline{9}$ $\overline{39}$

H. La parte intelectual
del hombre:

$\overline{17}$ $\overline{22}$ $\overline{2}$ $\overline{26}$ $\overline{37}$

ADIVINANZA PARA ADIVINAR:

1 D	2 H		3 A	4 G	5 C	6 D		7 B	8 B	9 G	10 G
11 A	12 E		13 B	14 D	15 A	16 C		17 H	18 C	19 D	20 B
21 E		22 H	23 C		24 F	25 B	26 H	27 A		28 C	29 G	30 B	31 E
	32 E	33 F		34 F	35 E	36 D	37 H	38 E	39 G	40 F	41 E	¿ ?

RESPUESTA: _____

38

¡ADIVINA, ADIVINADOR!

PALABRAS PARA ADIVINAR:

A. Pronombre relativo:

$\overline{3}$ $\overline{26}$ $\overline{1}$

B. Ninguna persona:

$\overline{15}$ $\overline{28}$ $\overline{21}$ $\overline{29}$ $\overline{11}$

C. Esposa del hijo,
   hija política:

$\overline{27}$ $\overline{4}$ $\overline{5}$ $\overline{18}$ $\overline{35}$

D. Diez por diez:

$\overline{23}$ $\overline{34}$ $\overline{7}$ $\overline{2}$

E. Lo opuesto de "delgado":

$\overline{30}$ $\overline{10}$ $\overline{14}$ $\overline{32}$ $\overline{33}$ $\overline{24}$

F. Reproducción de una carta
   o de una obra de arte:

$\overline{12}$ $\overline{20}$ $\overline{8}$ $\overline{22}$ $\overline{25}$

G. Forma de "leer" (3ª per.):

$\overline{31}$ $\overline{17}$ $\overline{13}$

H. Nación, patria:

$\overline{16}$ $\overline{9}$ $\overline{19}$ $\overline{6}$

ADIVINANZA PARA ADIVINAR:

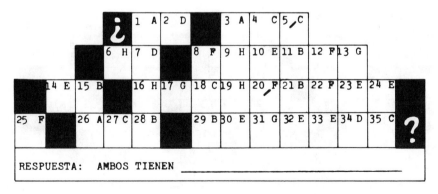

RESPUESTA: AMBOS TIENEN _____

¡ADIVINA, ADIVINADOR!

PALABRAS PARA ADIVINAR:

A. Los que forman el esqueleto
de los animales (pl.):

$\overline{14}$ $\overline{1}$ $\overline{5}$ $\overline{37}$ $\overline{20}$ $\overline{31}$

B. Insecto que teje su vivienda:

$\overline{3}$ $\overline{8}$ $\overline{30}$ $\overline{6}$ $\overline{40}$

C. Barco grande:

$\overline{10}$ $\overline{24}$ $\overline{23}$ $\overline{27}$ $\overline{36}$

D. Los dos extremos laterales
de la frente:

$\overline{21}$ $\overline{11}$ $\overline{34}$ $\overline{26}$ $\overline{17}$ $\overline{41}$

E. Comida que se toma
por la noche:

$\overline{16}$ $\overline{12}$ $\overline{28}$ $\overline{42}$

F. Los extremos móviles de las
manos y de los pies (pl.):

$\overline{19}$ $\overline{25}$ $\overline{35}$ $\overline{7}$ $\overline{4}$

G. Artículo indefinido (fem.):

$\overline{38}$ $\overline{2}$ $\overline{9}$

H. Un cabello blanco:

$\overline{29}$ $\overline{32}$ $\overline{13}$ $\overline{15}$

I. Tribu o familia en Escocia:

$\overline{39}$ $\overline{33}$ $\overline{22}$ $\overline{18}$

ADIVINANZA PARA ADIVINAR:

1 A	2 G	3 B		4 F	5 A	6 B	7 F	8 B	9 G		
10 C	11 D	12 E	13 H	14 A	15 H	16 E	17 D	18 I	19 F	20 A	21 D	22 I
23 C	24 C	25 F		26 D	27 C	28 E	29 H	30 B		31 A	32 H	33 I	34 D
	35 F	36 C		37 A	38 G		39 I	40 B	41 D	42 E	

RESPUESTA: _____

40

CITAS LITERARIAS

Juegos

para los expertos

VACAS Y SOGAS

Ésta es la sección más difícil del libro,
pero con un poco de paciencia y medita-
ción usted podrá resolver todos estos anagramas -- y un acróstico.

El procedimiento es el mismo de antes
pero ahora . . .

las primeras letras de
las palabras definidas
le darán el autor·de la
cita que resultará al final

A. El que no puede ver: C I E G O
$\overline{1}$ $\overline{10}$ $\overline{13}$ $\overline{37}$ $\overline{31}$

B. Pronombre femenino: E L L A
$\overline{8}$ $\overline{22}$ $\overline{33}$ $\overline{16}$

C. Mujer que tiene riquezas: $\overline{27}$ $\overline{21}$ $\overline{25}$ $\overline{42}$

D. Lo que hacen los
pájaros o los aviones: $\overline{17}$ $\overline{6}$ $\overline{23}$ $\overline{3}$ $\overline{12}$

E. Lo contrario de "allí": $\overline{18}$ $\overline{19}$ $\overline{38}$ $\overline{39}$

F. Lo contrario de
"siempre": $\overline{4}$ $\overline{2}$ $\overline{14}$ $\overline{30}$ $\overline{24}$

G. Paso subterráneo: $\overline{7}$ $\overline{20}$ $\overline{32}$ $\overline{29}$ $\overline{40}$

H. Artículo definido: $\overline{11}$ $\overline{41}$

I. El que suelda: $\overline{35}$ $\overline{26}$ $\overline{15}$ $\overline{5}$ $\overline{34}$ $\overline{9}$ $\overline{36}$ $\overline{28}$

Recuerde que las letras de unas palabras pueden ayudarle a adivinar otras letras.

Las casillas oscuras, dondequiera que estén, indican la separación de las palabras (por ejemplo, la palabra que empieza con 25-C continúa hasta 29-G)

CITA:

1 A	2 F	3 D	4 F	5 I	6 D		7 G	8 B	
C						■		E	■
9 I	10 A	11 H	12 D	13 A	14 F		15 I	16 B	
	I			E		■		A	■
17 D	18 E	19 E	20 G	21 C	22 B	23 D	24 F		25 C
				L				■	
26 I	27 C	28 I	29 G		30 F	31 A	32 G		33 B
				■		O		■	L
34 I		35 I	36 I	37 A	38 E	39 E	40 G	41 H	42 C
	■			G					

El autor de esta cita es muy famoso.

¿Quién es? _____

(Lea hacia abajo las primeras letras de las palabras definidas en la página anterior.)

43

Véase la muestra
en la página 42

CITA

MORALEJA DE UNA FÁBULA

A. En todo tiempo (adv.):	55 40 24 32 43 34 51
B. Forma masculina del adjetivo "aquella":	35 36 58 45 7
C. Sesenta segundos:	11 23 4 27 49 60
D. En este momento:	3 5 2 30 54
E. Forma posesiva del pronombre "nosotros":	17 29 6 9 28 59 13
F. Las personas que no son "fieles" son ---	10 1 26 33 50 42 56 46
G. Amoldar estatuas (con el pronombre "ellos"):	16 52 14 37 21 12 38 39
H. Dueño de una tienda o de una casa de comercio:	57 41 44 19 25 53 20
I. Forma de "obtener" con "él" (tiempo presente):	31 22 18 15 47 48 8

CITA:

1 F	2 D		3 D	4 C	5 D	6 E	7 B	8 I	9 E	
10 F	11 C	12 G	13 E	14 G	15 I	16 G	17 E	18 I	19 H	
20 H	21 G		22 I	23 C	24 A	25 H		26 F	27 C	28 E
29 E	30 D	31 I		32 A	33 F	34 A	35 B		36 B	37 G
38 G		39 G	40 A		41 H	42 F		43 A	44 H	45 B
46 F	47 I	48 I	49 C	50 F		51 A	52 G	53 H	54 D	
	55 A	56 F	57 H	58 B	59 E	60 C	

POEMA ANTIGUO

El autor de esta cita no es conocido, pero las primeras letras de las palabras definidas le darán el título famoso.

A. Cocer alimento:

$\overline{4}$ $\overline{16}$ $\overline{31}$ $\overline{49}$ $\overline{75}$ $\overline{77}$ $\overline{82}$

B. Tienda donde se
venden mercancías:

$\overline{6}$ $\overline{25}$ $\overline{57}$ $\overline{79}$ $\overline{48}$ $\overline{30}$ $\overline{67}$

C. Narraciones ficticias
muy populares:

$\overline{3}$ $\overline{45}$ $\overline{73}$ $\overline{70}$ $\overline{34}$ $\overline{56}$ $\overline{64}$

D. Vendedores de billetes
en las taquillas:

$\overline{7}$ $\overline{24}$ $\overline{28}$ $\overline{52}$ $\overline{11}$ $\overline{42}$ $\overline{59}$ $\overline{53}$ $\overline{62}$ $\overline{72}$ $\overline{85}$

E. Aeroplano:

$\overline{38}$ $\overline{37}$ $\overline{69}$ $\overline{84}$ $\overline{22}$

F. Líneas de luz que salen
de un cuerpo luminoso:

$\overline{8}$ $\overline{39}$ $\overline{46}$ $\overline{61}$ $\overline{65}$

G. Tener dudas:

$\overline{33}$ $\overline{41}$ $\overline{71}$ $\overline{74}$ $\overline{19}$

H. Preposición de lugar:

$\overline{14}$ $\overline{50}$

I. "Madre" en lenguaje
familiar o infantil:

$\overline{10}$ $\overline{43}$ $\overline{60}$ $\overline{76}$

J. Metal que atrae
a otros metales:

$\overline{21}$ $\overline{13}$ $\overline{81}$ $\overline{54}$

K. Escondidos:

$\overline{2}$ $\overline{80}$ $\overline{5}$ $\overline{35}$ $\overline{78}$ $\overline{9}$ $\overline{27}$

46

L. Parte del cuerpo que une la cabeza con el tronco (plural):

$$\overline{51}\ \overline{29}\ \overline{36}\ \overline{12}\ \overline{83}\ \overline{63}\ \overline{40}$$

M. Presente indicativo de "imitar" con "yo":

$$\overline{32}\ \overline{68}\ \overline{58}\ \overline{18}\ \overline{26}$$

N. Los doctores que cuidan los dientes:

$$\overline{44}\ \overline{20}\ \overline{15}\ \overline{55}\ \overline{66}\ \overline{1}\ \overline{23}\ \overline{47}\ \overline{17}$$

CITA:

	1 N	2 K	3 C		4 A	5 K	6 B	7 D	8 F	9 K	
10 I	11 D	12 L		13 J	14 H	15 N	16 A	17 N		18 M	19 G
20 N	21 J	22 E	23 N	24 D		25 B	26 M	27 K		28 D	29 L
30 B		31 A	32 M	33 G		34 C	35 K	36 L	37 E	38 E	
39 F		40 L	41 G		42 D	43 I	44 N	45 C		46 F	
47 N		48 B	49 A	50 H	51 L	52 D	53 D	54 J	55 N	56 C	
57 B	58 M	59 D		60 I	61 F	62 D	63 L	64 C		65 F	66 N
67 B		68 M	69 E	70 C	71 G	72 D		73 C	74 G	75 A	
76 I		77 A	78 K	79 B	80 K	81 J	82 A	83 L	84 E	85 D	

47

Véase la muestra
en la página 42

POETA SATÍRICO

A. Crepúsculo,
hacerse de noche: $\overline{7}$ $\overline{14}$ $\overline{17}$ $\overline{20}$ $\overline{21}$ $\overline{26}$ $\overline{40}$ $\overline{53}$ $\overline{72}$

B. El que repara
relojes: $\overline{57}$ $\overline{66}$ $\overline{74}$ $\overline{123}$ $\overline{77}$ $\overline{96}$ $\overline{113}$ $\overline{76}$

C. Documento
bancario: $\overline{3}$ $\overline{38}$ $\overline{55}$ $\overline{116}$ $\overline{43}$ $\overline{119}$

D. Alumbrar,
poner luces: $\overline{13}$ $\overline{32}$ $\overline{117}$ $\overline{50}$ $\overline{100}$ $\overline{45}$ $\overline{125}$ $\overline{52}$

E. Lo que necesita
solución, difi- $\overline{36}$ $\overline{126}$ $\overline{68}$ $\overline{88}$ $\overline{93}$ $\overline{103}$ $\overline{82}$ $\overline{105}$
cultad:

F. Hacer de nuevo: $\overline{120}$ $\overline{37}$ $\overline{48}$ $\overline{61}$ $\overline{67}$ $\overline{101}$ $\overline{30}$

G. Felicitación,
felizmente: $\overline{15}$ $\overline{106}$ $\overline{63}$ $\overline{78}$ $\overline{91}$ $\overline{73}$ $\overline{42}$ $\overline{19}$ $\overline{71}$ $\overline{111}$ $\overline{87}$

H. Ausencia de agua,
acritud de $\overline{24}$ $\overline{58}$ $\overline{94}$ $\overline{95}$ $\overline{112}$ $\overline{25}$ $\overline{80}$ $\overline{109}$
carácter:

I. Distancia,
espacio de tiempo: $\overline{33}$ $\overline{69}$ $\overline{92}$ $\overline{65}$ $\overline{86}$ $\overline{98}$

J. Ocupaciones: $\overline{23}$ $\overline{28}$ $\overline{56}$ $\overline{81}$ $\overline{121}$ $\overline{49}$ $\overline{115}$

K. Pérdida del sentido,
desfallecimiento: $\overline{54}$ $\overline{9}$ $\overline{59}$ $\overline{104}$ $\overline{90}$ $\overline{79}$ $\overline{85}$

L. El que elige: $\overline{10}$ $\overline{11}$ $\overline{41}$ $\overline{8}$ $\overline{122}$ $\overline{5}$ $\overline{16}$

M. Bello, que tiene
hermosura: $\overline{4}$ $\overline{44}$ $\overline{35}$ $\overline{124}$ $\overline{46}$ $\overline{108}$ $\overline{22}$

N. No habitado,
desierto: $\overline{110}$ $\overline{97}$ $\overline{6}$ $\overline{27}$ $\overline{51}$ $\overline{118}$ $\overline{99}$ $\overline{29}$ $\overline{84}$ $\overline{107}$

O. Originario
de Troya: $\overline{60}$ $\overline{62}$ $\overline{114}$ $\overline{47}$ $\overline{31}$ $\overline{102}$ $\overline{34}$

P. Juntar, reunir: $\overline{39}$ $\overline{75}$ $\overline{2}$ $\overline{18}$ $\overline{83}$ $\overline{89}$ $\overline{64}$ $\overline{70}$

CITA:

■	1 X **M**	2 P	3 C	4 M	5 L	■	6 N	7 A	8 L	9 K
■	10 L	11 L	■	12 X **D**	13 D	14 A	15 G	16 L	17 A	■
18 P	19 G	20 A	21 A	22 M	■	23 J	24 H	■	25 H	26 A
■	27 N	28 J	29 N	30 F	■	31 O	32 D	■	33 I	34 O
35 M	36 E	37 F	■	38 C	39 P	40 A	41 L	■	42 G	43 C
44 M	45 D	46 M	■	47 O	■	48 F	49 J	50 D	51 N	52 D
53 A	■	54 K	55 C	■	56 J	57 B	58 H	59 K	60 O	61 F
62 O	■	63 G	64 P	65 I	66 B	■	67 F	68 E	69 I	70 P
71 G	72 A	■	73 G	74 B	■	75 P	76 B	77 B	78 G	■
79 K	■	80 H	81 J	■	82 E	83 P	84 N	85 K	■	86 I
87 G	88 E	89 P	90 K	91 G	■	92 I	93 E	■	94 H	95 H
96 B	■	97 N	98 I	■	99 N	100 D	101 F	102 O	103 E	■
104 K	105 E	106 G	107 N	108 M	■	109 H	110 N	111 G	112 H	113 B
■	114 O	115 J	■	116 C	117 D	118 N	119 C	120 F	121 J	
■	■	122 L	123 B	124 M	125 D	126 E	■			

- A -

aborigen--aboriginal, native
abreviar--to abbreviate
la abreviatura--abbreviation
el abuelo--grandfather
la acritud--sourness
actualmente--at present,at
  the present time
acumular--to accumulate
el adagio--adage, wise
  saying
la adivinanza--riddle
adivinar--to guess, see
  through
agarrar--to grasp
el agua--water
la aguja--needle
ahogar--to drown, choke,
  smother
ahora--now
ahora mismo--right now
ahornar--to bake
la alacena--cupboard
algún, alguno--some, any
el alimento--food
allí--there, over there
el almacén--store
alto,-a--high, tall
alumbrar--to illuminate,
  give light
alumno, -a--pupil
amar--to love
amarillo-yellow
el amor--love
el anaquel--shelf
anciano, -a--old
anhelar--to covet
anoche--last night
los anteojos--eye glasses
anterior--preceding, front
antes (de) -- before
el año--year
el aparato--device, set
el apodo--nickname
aprender--to learn
  aprender de memoria--to
  memorize
apuntar--to aim (a firearm)
aquellos--those
aquí--here
la araña--spider
el árbol--tree
el armario--wardrobe,closet
arriba--up, upward
el arroz--rice
el artículo--article
atacar (qu)--to attack
el ateo--atheist
la ausencia--absence

el autor--author
la autoridad--authority
el ave--bird
el avión--airplane
ayer--yesterday
ayudar--to aid, assist

- B -

la bahía--bay
balar--to bleat
el banco--bank
bancario, -a--bank, pertain-
  ing to a bank
bañarse--to bathe
baño--bath
barato, -a--cheap
el barco--boat, ship
el bastón--cane, walking
  stick
el baúl--trunk
el bebé--child
beber--to drink
bello,-a--beautiful
la boca--mouth
el bocado--mouthful, bite
la bolsa--sack, purse
breve--brief
el brindis--toast (to a
  person's health)
bueno, -a--good
el buque--ship
buscar--to look for, seek
el buzo--frogman

- C -

el caballo--horse
el cabello--hair
caer (irr.)--to fall
el camino--road, way; el
  camino real--main
  road, highway
la campana--bell
el can (perro)--dog
la cana--gray hair
la capa--cape
el cariño--affection,
  fondness
la carta--letter
la casa--house
casado, -a(con)--married(to)
casarse--to get married,
  to marry; casar con--to
  marry someone to
la cavidad--cavity
la ceja--brow, eyebrow
la cena--supper
cenar--to have supper
cero--zero

el cerdo--pig
el cetro--scepter, staff
ciego, -a--blind
el cielo--sky, heaven
cien(to)--a one hundred
la cima--top, summit
cincuenta--fifty
la cita--quotation
la ciudad--city
el ciudadano--citizen
el clan--clan
cocinar--to cook
cojo--lame
la cola--tail
comenzar(ie;c)--to begin,
  start
comer--to eat; como--I eat
la comida--meal, dinner
compañero,-a--companion
la compra--buy, purchase
comprar--to buy
la conquista--conquest
la copia--copy
cortar--to cut
correr--to run
coser--to sew
creer(y)--to believe
cuando--when
¿cuánto,-a?--how much?
cuatro--four
culpable--guilty, be to
  blame

- CH -

el cheque--check

- D -

dar(irr.)--to give, grant
debajo--under, beneath
de nuevo--again
decir(irr.)--to say, tell
el dedo--finger
definido, -a--defined
definir--to define
del(de+el)--of the
delgado,-a--thin
derecho,-a--right
  a la derecha--at the right
descubrir--to discover
desear--to desire, want
el desfallecimiento--swoon,
  faintness
desierto,-a--desert, de-
  serted, uninhabited
desmayarse--to faint, swoon
el desmayo--faint, weakness
detenerse--to stop
  ¡Detente!--(command)stop!
la deuda--debt
el día--day
el diente--tooth

dieren--future subjunctive
  of dar
diez--ten
el dinero--money
Dios--God
la distancia--distance
doce--twelve
dondequiera--wherever
dudar--to doubt
el Duero--river in central
  Spain and Portugal
el duque--duke
la duquesa--duchess
- E -

echar--to throw, cast
la edad--age
EE.UU.--U.S.A.
la elección--choice, elec-
  tion
elegir--to choose, elect
elevar--to elevate, raise
ella--she
en--in, into, at, on,within
encontrar(ue)--to find, en-
  counter, meet
ene--name of the letter "n"
la enhorabuena--congratula-
  tions
entre--among, between
errar--to err
la escala--scale
esconder--hide
escribir--to write
el espacio--space
  —de tiempo--span of time
esposo,-a--spouse
la esquela--note
estos--these
estudiar--to study
- F -

faltar--to be lacking
la felicitación--congratu-
  lation
feliz(pl. felices)--happy
felizmente--happily
la flor--flower
la frase--phrase
el fuego--fire
fuerte--strong
fumar--to smoke
- G -

la gallina--hen
el gallo--rooster
ganar--to win, gain
la ganga--bargain
gatear--to crawl
gato,-a--cat
la Giralda--weather vane
  and tower of the cathe-
  dral of Sevilla
la gente--people

el gobierno--government
la gota--drop
grande--big, large
grueso,-a--thick, heavy
el guante--glove
la guerra--war
gustar--to be pleasing

- H -

habitar--to inhabit
hacendoso,-a--diligent,
 industrious
hacer(irr.)--to make, do
 hacerse--to become, to
 get; hacerse de noche--
 to become night, to get
 dark
hallar--to find
el hambre--hunger
hambriento--starving
la harina--flour
hay que--it is necessary,
 must
he de + inf.--I will + inf.
la hebra--piece of thread
la hembra--female
la herida--wound
hermoso,-a--beautiful
la hija--daughter

el hijo--son
la hoja--leaf
el hombre--man
 hombre de prestar--useful
 man
la hora--hour, time
el hueso--bone
el huevo--egg
el humo--smoke

- I -

iluminado,-a --illuminated
iluminar--to illuminate,
 to light (up)
el imán--magnet
imperativo--imperative
 (command) form
indeciso,-a--hesitant,
 irresolute
el inglés--English(language)
ir(irr.)--to go
la izquierda--left

- J -

el juego--game, play
el juguete--toy
junio--June
juntar--to join, unite
junto a--near, next to

- L -

el lado--side, direction
lavar--to wash
la lectura--reading
leer(y)--to read
la lengua--tongue, language
el lenguaje--language
los lentes--eye glasses,
 lenses
la letra--letter (of
 alphabet)
la ley-law
la leyenda--legend
el libro--book
 el librito--little book

lindo,-a--pretty
el líquido--liquid
liviano,-a--light (in
 weight)
la locomotora--locomotive
luego--soon, then, next
el lugar--place, village
el lujo--luxury
el lunes--Monday
la luz--light

- LL -

la llaga--wound, sore
llamar--to call, summon
llenar--to fill
lleno,-a--full
llevar--to carry, take
llorar--to cry, weep
la lluvia--rain

- M -

el machete--machete, large
 knife
el macho--male (usually
 animals)
la madre--mother
la maestra--teacher
la maleta--bag, valise
mamá--Mom
mandar--to order, ask, send
la manga--sleeve
el mango--mango (tropical
 fruit)
la mano--hand
el(la) mar--sea, ocean
el marido--husband
el maya--Maya, Mayan
mayo--May
me (pronoun)--me, to me,
 myself, to myself
mejor--better, best
menos--less, least
la mente--mind
mentiroso,-a--liar

el mes--month
el miedo--fear
mil--(a or one) thousand
mirar--to look, look at
mismo, -a--same, very
la montaña--mountain
morar--to dwell, reside
morir(se)--to die
el moro--Moor
el mozo--lad, youth
el muchacho--boy
mudo, -a--silent, mute
muere--see: morir
la muestra--sample
la mujer--woman, wife
el mundo--world, everybody

- N -

nadar--to swim
nadie--no one
la nana--grandma
narrar--to narrate, relate
la natación--swimming
navegar--to navigate, sail
negro, -a--black
el(la) nene--baby
ni--neither, nor
   ni...ni....--neither...nor
el nido--nest
el nieto--grandson, grand-
   child
ningún, ninguno, -a--not
   any (adj.)
el niño--boy, child
la noche--night
de noche--at night
el nombre--name
el norte--north
la nube--cloud
la nuera--daughter-in-law
nuevo, -a--new
el número--number
nunca--never

- O -

oculto, -a--hidden
el odio--hatred
oír--to hear
el ojo--eye
la oración--sentence, prayer
orar--to pray
originario,-a--native,
   originating
la osa--female bear; Osa
   Menor (astr.)--Little
   Bear; Osa Mayor(astr.)--
   Great Bear
oscuro,-a--dark (blackened)
el oso--bear (male)
la oveja--sheep
el(la) oyente--listener, hearer

la paciencia--patience
el padre--father,(pl.)
   parents
el país--country, land
el pájaro--bird
la palabra--word, promise
el pan--bread
el papel--paper
parecido,-a--like, similar
el parque--park
pasar--to pass, go on
el paseo--walk
la pata--leg (& foot) of
   animal; female duck
el pato--male duck
pelar--to cut the hair off,
   to pluck the feathers
   from, to peel
la pelea--fight
pelirrojo,-a--red-haired
pensar--to think
peor--worse, worst
pequeño,-a--small, little
percibir--to perceive with
   the senses
perdedor--loser
perder--to lose
la pérdida--loss
el perro--dog
el personaje--personage,
   character(in a play or
   novel)
pesado,-a--heavy
pescado--fish that has
   been caught
el pez--fish
el pie--foot
   al pie--at the foot, at
   the bottom
la piel--skin
   pieles rojas--red skins
pierde--see perder
pintar--to paint
el piñón--pine kernel
la pipa--pipe
el plomo--lead
la población--population
poco,-a--little
   pocos, -as--few
poder--to be able (to)
podrá--future form of poder
la poesía--poetry, poem
el poeta--poet
el pollo--chicken, young
   cock
poner--to put, place
porque--because, so that
la prenda--garment, article
   of clothing
primer(o),-a--first

primo,-a--cousin
el procedimiento--method,
  procedure
el puerco--pig, hog
puso--(poner) he, she put

- Q -

que(rel.pro.)--that, which,
  who, whom
¿qué?--what?, which?
quemar--to burn
querer--to want, wish, love
quien(quienes,pl.)--who
Quito--capital of Ecuador

- R -

el rabo--tail
rajar--to split, crack
la rama--branch
la rata--rat
el rayo--ray, lightning
recordar--to recall, re-
  member
el recreo--entertainment,
  recreation
recuerde--(command)
  remember; see recordar
regalar--to give, present
regalado--given
la regla--rule, regulation
rehacer--to remake, make
  over
la reina--queen
el relato--report, account,
  story
el reloj--watch
  relojero--watchmaker
repaso--review
resolver(ue)--to resolve,
  solve
la respuesta--answer
el resultado--result,
  yield
reunir--to collect, present
el rey--king
rico,-a--rich
los rieles--railway tracks
la rifa--sweepstakes
el río--river
la riqueza--wealth, rich-
  ness
el roedor--rodent
rojo,-a--red
romper--to break, cut
  through
la ropa--clothing
la rosa--rose
rubio,-a--blond, blonde
el ruido--noise, sound

- S -

el sábado--Saturday
sacar--extract, get, obtain
la sala--room, sitting room
  la sala de clase--class-
  room
salir--to leave, go out
San--short for Santo-saint
  (used before masculine
  names)
se--(obj.pron.) to him, to
  her, to you, to them;
  (reflex. pron.) himself,
  herself, themselves, your-
  self
seguir--to follow, continue
según--according to, as
segundo,-a--second
la semana--week
el sentido--sense, feeling;
  perder el sentido--to
  pass out
señalar--to point out,
  indicate
el señor--sir, Mr,gentleman
la señora--lady, madam, Mrs.
la sequedad--dryness
ser(irr.)--to be, exist
  será--future form of ser
servir--to serve
siempre--always
la sien--temple (of the forehead)
siete--seven
sigue--see seguir
siguiente--following, next
sobrenombre--nickname
la soguilla--(diminutive of
  soga)--little rope,string
el soldador--welder
subterráneo,-a--subterran-
  ean, underground
Suecia--Sweden
sueca--Swedish woman
la suelda--welding
el suelo--ground, floor
la suerte--luck, lot
la suspicacia--suspicious-
  ness, distrust
el sustantivo--noun

- T -

la tabla--board, plank
el tambor--drum
tampoco--neither
taquillero,-a--ticket
  seller
la tarde--afternoon
¡tate!--(command) take care!,
  beware!

54

la techumbre--roof
la tejedora--weaver
tejer--to weave
tener(irr.)--to have, own,
  possess
la tía--aunt
la tienda--store
tierno,-a--tender, young
tirar--to draw, pull
tocar--to touch, play
  (music)
todo,-a--all, whole, every
tomar--to take, pick up,
  eat, drink
tonto,-a--foolish, silly
la topinera--mole-hill
la tormenta--storm
torpe--awkward, dull,
  stupid
la torre--tower
trabajar--to work, toil,
  labor
transferir--to transfer
tratarse de--to be a
  question of
el trecho--space, distance
el tren--train
la tropa--troop
Troya--Troy; troyano--
  Trojan
el trueno--thunder, thunder-
  clap
tu, tus--your, yours (fam.)
el túnel--tunnel

- U -

un(o), -a--one; unos, -as--
  some, several
usar--to use, employ
usted(Ud.)--you(formal)
el utensillo--utensil
la uva--grape

- V -

el vagón--railway car,coach
valer--to be worth, be val-
  uable
la valija--valise, satchel
el valle--valley
la vaquilla--diminutive of
  vaca, little cow
el vaso--glass, vase
la vela--sail, candle
ver--to see
vestir--to dress, wear
el viaje--trip
viejo,-a--old, ancient
el vino--wine
vivir--to live, be alive
volar--to fly
la voz--voice

- Y -

ya--already, now
  ya no--no longer
el yate--yacht
yerra--see errar

ENGLISH - SPANISH

- A -

a--un, una
accumulate--acumular
age--la edad
airplane--el avión
always--siempre
and--y
atheist--el ateo

- B -

baby--el bebé, el (la) nene
bad--malo
badly--mal
bag--la bolsa
bargain--la ganga
bark--el ladrido
bath--el baño
bay--la bahía
be--ser, estar
bear--oso,-a
beautiful--hermoso, -a
  bello, -a

beware-- ¡tate!
black--negro, -a
blind--ciego, -a
boy--el muchacho
branch--la rama
bread--el pan
break--romper, quebrar
Buddha--Buda
bullet--la bala
burn--quemar

- C -

candle--la vela
cape--la capa
cat--el gato
chicken--el pollo
city--la ciudad
clan--el clan
classroom--la sala de clase
command--mandar
cook--cocinar
congratulation--la
  enhorabuena

copy--la copia
country--el país
cradle--la cuna
cry--llorar

- D -

darken (grow dark)--ano-
  checer
daughter-in-law--la nuera
dismay--el desmayo
distance--el trecho
diver--el buzo
dog--el perro, el can
doubt--dudar
drink--beber
dryness--la sequedad
duchess--la duquesa

- E -

elect--elegir
elector--el elector
eyebrow--la ceja

- F -

face--la cara
fall--caer
fifteen--quince
find--hallar
finger--el dedo
fly--volar
for--para, por
four--cuatro
from--de
fruit--la fruta
full--lleno, -a

- G -

gather--acumular
girl--la muchacha
give--dar
glasses--lentes
glove--el guante
go--ir (voy)
grandfather--el abuelo
grandmother--la abuela
grandson--el nieto
grape--la uva

- H -

hair--el pelo (gray--la cana)
hate--el odio
hear--oír
hearer--el oyente
heavy--pesado, -a
here--aquí
hidden--escondido, -a;
  oculto, -a
his--su

honeymoon--la luna de miel
hour--la hora

- I -

in--dentro de, en
is--es, está; hace (weather)
illuminate--iluminar

- J -

January--el enero
jaw--la quijada
job--el empleo

- L -

lagoon--la laguna
last night--anoche
law--la ley
lenses--los lentes
light--iluminar
like--gustar, querer
listener--el oyente
lose--perder
loser--el perdedor
love--querer, amar
lover--el amante
luck--la suerte

- M -

magnet--el imán
mail--el correo
mama--mamá
manager--el gerente
mind--la mente
minute--el minuto
Monday--el lunes
monitor - el monitor
moon--la luna
month--el mes
my--mi, mis

- N -

N--ene
neither--ni
nest--el nido
never--nunca
nickname--el apodo
nobody--nadie
noise--el ruido
nor--ni
note--la esquela
nothing--nada, cero
novel--la novela
now--ahora

- O -

obtain--obtener
occupation--el empleo

old--viejo, -a
our--nuestro, -a

- P -

paper--el papel
park--el parque
peel--pelar
people--la gente
peso (Mexican coin)--el
  peso
pig--el cerdo, el puerco
pipe--la pipa
please--por favor
poet--el poeta
pray--orar
problem--el problema
purse--la bolsa

- Q -

queen--la reina

- R -

rail--el riel
rat--la rata
ray--el rayo
read--leer
reading--la lectura
red--rojo, -a
redo (do again)--rehacer
redheaded--pelirrojo, -a
review--el repaso
rich--rico, -a
roof--la techumbre, el tejado
rooster--el gallo
rose--la rosa
royal--real

- S -

saint--el santo (san)
Saturday--el sábado
say--decir
scepter--el cetro
sculpt--esculpir
sea--el (la) mar
see--ver
set (table)--poner
seven--siete
ship--el buque
sky--el cielo
snow--la nieve
sore--la llaga
south--sur, sud
spider--la araña
store--el almacén
student--el estudiante
stupid--tonto, -a
suitcase--la valija
summit--la cima

supper--la cena
Swede--el sueco
swim--nadar

- T -

tail--la cola
teach--enseñar
temple (forehead)--la sien
than--que
that (adj.)--aquel, -la
these (adj.)--estos, -as
those (adj.)--aquellos,-as
thousand--mil
thread--el hilo
thunder--el trueno
ticketseller--el taquillero
time--el tiempo, la hora
topic--el asunto, el tema
toward--hacia
towel--la toalla
tower--la torre
toy--el juguete
train--el tren
trip--el viaje
troop--la tropa
tunnel--el túnel

- U -

unfaithful--infiel
Ursa Major (constellation)
  -- Osa Mayor
U.S.A. -- EE.UU.or E.U.

- V -

valley--el valle
voyage--el viaje

- W -

waist--el talle
war--la guerra
was--era
wash--lavar
watchmaker--el relojero
weigh--pesar
welder--el soldador
with--con
world--el mundo
wound--la llaga

- Y -

yacht--el yate
year--el año
yolk--la yema

- Z -

zero--el cero

ANSWER KEY

MUESTRA ILUSTRATIVA (Page 1)

1. baño
2. halla
3. pesa
4. que
5. sí

Welcome sign for Spanish-speaking people abroad:

Aquí se habla español.

¡NO LO CREO! (Page 2)

1. ocho
2. osa
3. enero
4. suerte
5. por

Tell that to somebody else!

¡A otro perro con ese hueso!

¡FIESTA! (Page 3)

1. hacia
2. luna
3. cara
4. en
5. era

Have a fling, go on a spree:

Echar una cana al aire.

OTRA COSA (Page 4)

1. sala
2. hace
3. torre
4. osos
5. tenido

That's something else again!

¡Eso es harina de otro costal!

INEPTO (Page 5)

1. bolsa
2. Camino
3. roja
4. manda
5. ni

To run around in circles:

Andar como bola sin manija.

¡PRONTO! (Page 6)

1. aquellos
2. con
3. mundo
4. gatean
5. leen

In less time than it takes

En menos de lo que canta un gallo.

MUY INCÓMODO (Page 7)

1. guante, en
2. moreno
3. pesado
4. lectura
5. repaso

To be very much out of place:

Estar como un gato en una pelea de perros. (Colombia)

SUSPICACIA (Page 8)

1. hora
2. rey
3. Quien
4. Cada
5. gota

Something rotten in Denmark:

Aquí hay gato encerrado.

HAMBRIENTO (Page 9)

1. nene
2. Costa
3. ruido
4. lleno
5. leer
6. ora

Hungry as a wolf (in Perú):

Estarle (a uno) corriendo el león.

EXAGERACIÓN (Page 10)

1. gato
2. nada
3. EE.UU.
4. se
5. ganga
6. hora

Make a big thing out of nothing:

Ahogarse en una gota de agua.

EXAGERACIÓN NICARAGÜENSE
(Page 11)

1. muchacha
2. en
3. juguete
4. era
5. nada

Mountain out of a molehill:

Hacer de una aguja un machete.
(Nicaragua)

¡CULPABLE!
(Page 12)

1. correo
2. llora
3. mango
4. "nana"
5. esquela

Catch a culprit in the act:

Agarrarlo con el queso en la mano.
(Venezuela)

LA PURA VERDAD
(Page 13)

1. voy
2. lavan
3. polla
4. rama
5. ni . . . ni
6. plan

To tell it the way it is—

Llamar al pan pan y al vino vino.

BRINDIS A LA ESPAÑOLA
(Page 14)

1. pesos
2. sala
3. de
4. mar
5. tu
6. y

A toast in Spanish:

Salud, pesetas y amor.

MERECIDO
(Page 15)

1. luna
2. rata
3. cielo
4. Perro
5. Luis
6. toalla

To have something backfire:

Salirle (a uno) el tiro por la culata.

BUEN SENTIDO
(Page 16)

A. cejas
B. quemar
C. den
D. trueno

Another version of *"Más vale tarde que nunca"* (See p. 1):

Mejor es tarde que nunca.

PESCADO
(Page 17)

A. me
B. se
C. pelar
D. buzo
E. puerco

Proverb: Por su boca muere el pez.

PENSAMIENTO
(Page 18)

A. bebé
B. apodo
C. quijada
D. cero
E. vela

Proverb: Oveja que bala pierde bocado.

DIVISA PARA ESTUDIANTES *(Page 19)*

A. querer
B. tema
C. balas
D. ven
E. se

Proverb: Más vale saber que tener.

HABLADOR
(Page 20)

A. hilo
B. muchacho
C. un
D. quebrar
E. yema

Proverb: Quien mucho habla, mucho yerra.

AVARICIA
(Page 21)

A. Quito
B. Perú
C. cima
D. rabo
E. capa
F. anoche

Proverb: Quien mucho abarca, poco aprieta.

DONDE HAY HUMO, HAY FUEGO
(Page 22)

A. rosa
B. poeta
C. reina
D. lunes
E. ciudad
F. re

Proverb: Cuando el río suena piedras trae.

RECUERDE (Page 23)

A. duquesa
B. di
C. Duero
D. llaga
E. maya

Proverb: Al que madruga, Dios le ayuda.

VENTAJA (Page 24)

A. siete
B. guerra
C. cetro
D. oyente
E. rieles
F. del

Proverb: En tierra de ciegos el tuerto es el rey.

TRISTE VERDAD (Page 25)

A. bello
B. estudiante
C. Vd.
D. viejo
E. ver
F. yate
G. votos

Proverb: El vivo vive del tonto y este de su trabajo.

NUNCA DIGAS NUNCA (Page 26)

A. negro
B. edad
C. gente
D. en
E. bahía
F. Buda
G. suecas

Proverb: Nunca digas de esta agua no he de beber.

CINISMO (Page 27)

A. quince
B. enseña
C. pierde
D. monitores
E. nieto

Proverb: Quien tiene dineros tiene compañeros.

MALOS COMPAÑEROS (Pages 28-29)

A. junio
B. abuelo
C. año
D. can
E. lentes
F. que
G. San
H. ser
I. al

Proverb: Quien con lobo se junta a aullar se enseña.

GRATITUD (Pages 30-31)

A. leyes
B. gallo
C. boca
D. tren
D. mina
E. ahora
G. esquela
H. ladrido

Proverb: A caballo regalado no hay que mirarle los dientes.

SABIDURÍA (Pages 32-33)

A. sábado
B. pollo
C. beber
D. parques
E. viaje
F. mil
G. odio

Proverb: Más sabe el diablo por viejo que por diablo.

MALA INVERSIÓN (Pages 34-35)

A. querer
B. nene
C. papel
D. yo
E. Diana
F. ene
G. pipa
H. pelirroja
I. perdedor

Proverb: Quien da pan a perro ajeno pierde el pan y pierde el perro.

¡ADIVINA, ADIVINADOR! (Page 36)

A. tejado
B. talle
C. nieve
D. nido
E. amante
F. cuna
G. laguna

Riddle: Una vieja con un diente llama a toda la gente.
(Answer: La campana)

¡ADIVINA, ADIVINADOR! (Page 37)

A. pan
B. das
C. san
D. Costa
E. tus
F. y
G. apaches
H. tropas
I. tate

Riddle: Tres patos y dos patas, ¿cuántas patas hacen?
(Answer: Doce patas—diez patas [feet] y dos patas [female ducks])

¡ADIVINA, ADIVINADOR!   *(Page 38)*

A. ateo
B. valija
C. tonto
D. reloj
E. leyenda
F. rata
G. elevo
H. mente

Riddle: En alto vive, en alto mora, y en
alto teje la tejedora.
(Answer: La araña)

¡ADIVINA, ADIVINADOR!   *(Page 39)*

A. que
B. nadie
C. nuera
D. cien
E. grueso
F. copia
G. lee
H. país

Riddle: ¿En qué se parece un periódico
a una iglesia?
(Answer: Ambos tienen columnas.)

¡ADIVINA, ADIVINADOR!   *(Page 40)*

A. huesos
B. araña
C. buque
D. sienes
E. cena
F. dedos
G. una
H. cana
I. clan

Riddle: Una señora bien hacendosa que
nunca sale de su casa.
(Answer: La tortuga)

VACAS Y SOGAS   *(Pages 42-43)*

A. ciego
B. ella
C. rica
D. volar
E. aquí
F. nunca
G. túnel
H. el
I. soldador

Quotation: Cuando te dieren la vaquilla,
corre con la soguilla.

Author: Miguel de CERVANTES
(1547-1616), author of *Don Quijote*

This quote is a good example of the many
wise sayings of Cervantes which have
become "proverbs" in their own right.

MORALEJA DE UNA FÁBULA
(Pages 44-45)

A. siempre
B. aquel
C. minuto
D. ahora
E. nuestra
F. infieles
G. esculpen
H. gerente
I. obtiene

Quotation: No anheles, impaciente, el
bien futuro. Mira que ni el
presente está seguro.

Author: Félix María de SAMANIEGO
(1745-1801), Basque, author of
Fábulas morales, fables in verse
which end with morals such as
this one.

POEMA ANTIGUO   *(Pages 46-47)*

A. cocinar
B. almacén
C. novelas
D. taquilleros
E. avión
F. rayos
G. dudar
H. en
I. mamá
J. imán
K. ocultos
L. cuellos
M. imito
N. dentistas

Quotation: Son cuatro mil menos treinta
los que Cid lleva a su lado y a
cincuenta mil moros sin
miedo van a atacarlos.

Source: *CANTAR DE MÍO CID*
First important literary work of
Spain (13th century) describing
the mighty deeds of the Cid
against fantastic odds such as
those quoted.

POETA SATÍRICO   *(Pages 48-49)*

A. anochecer
B. relojero
C. cheque
D. iluminar
E. problema
F. rehacer
G. enhorabuena
H. sequedad
I. trecho
J. empleos
K. desmayo
L. elector
M. hermoso
N. inhabitado
O. troyano
P. acumular

Quotation: Mucho hace el dinero,
Mucho es de amar:
Al torpe hace bueno
Y hombre de prestar
Hace correr al cojo
Y al mudo hablar,
El que no tiene manos,
Dineros quiere tomar.

Author: Juan Ruíz, ARCIPRESTE DE
HITA, Spain's greatest medieval
poet. (1283?-1350?), author of
El libro de buen amor.

61